Meeting God
at Midnight

Poems by
Ahuva Batya Scharff

Sociosights Press

Meeting God at Midnight

Poems by
Ahuva Batya Scharff

Sociosights Press

Other Books by the Author

Ending Addiction for Good
(written under the name,
Constance Scharff,
with Richard Taite)

Printed in the United States of America
First edition, 2014

Back cover photo: Ginny Belofsky

Book Orders: www.sociosights.com

Requests for permission to reproduce material from
this work should be sent to:
Sociosights Press
1402 Crestwood Road
Austin, TX 78722

136 pages (ppb)

ISBN 978-0-9916327-2-5

To Rabbi Neil
For helping me find hope
even in the darkness

Acknowledgements

It is with deepest gratitude that I thank those who helped me put this book together. Neena Husid and Cindy Huyser were amazing editors. My publisher and friend Devorah Winegarten has supported my efforts from the beginning. Rick Goldberg's assistance with matters of transliteration consistency and term accuracy was critical. And of course, Rabbi Neil Blumofe, to whom this book is dedicated, asked me, in the depths of my sadness, to write something for him every day; this is the beautiful work that is the end result.

Meeting God at Midnight

Table of Contents

The Jewish Mother Who Wasn't

The Jewish Mother Who Wasn't

Sara prayed for children and was sent Yitzhak.

Hana prayed for sons and was given Shmuel.

Rachel prayed and was rewarded, as was Rivkah.

In the Bible, all the women who pray for children

are heard and answered, except for Michal,

who remains barren not because HaShem shuns her,

but because David does.

What is wrong with me, God

that my prayers fall on deaf ears?

Why not allow me the greatest of all gifts,

the opportunity to be a mother?

Grain Silo: 1980

I climbed to the top of the grain silo and
sat on the ladder's highest rung.

I looked around.

Eight years old, *I couldn't quite tell*
if the silo was two or three stories tall.

To me, *it was enormous,*
by far the tallest structure on the farm.

I looked down. There was only hard-packed earth below.

Was I high enough to die, or would I only
break my legs and back?

I had a simple logic.

God refused to intervene *against my father.*

I begged for His help daily.

I would take matters into my own hands.

Dead, my father couldn't hurt me.

I stood up, *balancing carefully.*

"Conchita!" I heard my name shouted in Spanish.

It was Julien, our lead farm worker.

"Get down from there," he pleaded, running toward me.

I leaned back against the silo.

I liked Julien. There was no way I could hurt him by killing myself right before his eyes.

I climbed down, my first suicide attempt foiled.

Later that night, my father raped me again.

All I could do was cry.

Maimonides

You can't take back the kavanah
with which you imbue
an object or person.
You can't undo
a blessing or a curse.

How Esav howled
when Isaac gave the blessing
intended for him
to his brother, Jacob.
How I weep when
I reap the consequences
of the curses
my parents
have bequeathed.

Maimonides wrote
that we must burn even a Torah
written by one dispossessed
of the appropriate piety.
The scroll, he argued, becomes imbued
with the malevolence of the scribe,
just as people are inculcated
with the poison of the words
spoken over them.

What then for Esav?

What then for me?

No mikveh or prayer

can undo the wrong done.

Is there no path, HaShem,

back to wholeness?

After all it is not the scroll's

fault that it is unclean.

Bless Even Me

1.

Esav's wail reverberates in heaven,
his acid rain tears
forcing the angels to take cover
lest they be burned as the sky exploded
in the downpour of a man's anguish.

Howling with sadness
and the bitterness of betrayal,
Esav cries, "Bless me too, even me, Father!"
Calling out though there was no hope
of consolation or redemption.

What pain a man endures,
tricked out of his destiny,
by a brother and a mother
who favored another son.

2.

I remember the day my mother
traded my future for her freedom.

Gathering her purse and keys,
she said, "I'm taking Mikey. I'll be back later."
I was in bed with my father,
watching cartoons.

With my eyes, I begged, "Take me too."
She knew what he would do to me.
What mother wouldn't?
A crooked smile turned her face cold
as she tightened the grip on her keys.
Slowly she shook her head.

That day too the angels
had to take cover
from a downpour of acid tears.

Morning and Night

Night is the most difficult time,
when another day has passed
without any of my aspirations taking root.
I imagine you with me.
I am standing in the shul,
your arms around me,
giving the same comfort to me
you provide to all mourners.
Crying a little harder,
I can almost smell your distinct smell
and hear the soft cooing sound
you sometimes make
to those who are the most inconsolable.

When the day is new and full of hope,
it is his name that is first off my lips.
I wake up screaming,
terrified that he is coming for me,
not yet awake enough to know where I am
or that he is nearly seventeen years dead.

Once awake, I lie back into those same pillows
I held close the previous night,
breathing hard and trying to believe
that today will be a different sort of day.

I Want to Dance

I stand beside my rabbi
on the bimah at our shul.
We are standing to the side, talking,
though probably twenty other people are here.

The rabbi looks at me and says,
"I want to dance with you."
He has a big, expectant grin on his face,
showing the sincerity of his request.
"Mosh pit?" I query back.
"No. I want to dance."

I imagine him holding me.
My left hand in his right,
his hand on my waist,
mine on his shoulders,
preparing to waltz.

My heart squeezes with a shudder.
I want to dance, but I cannot.
He would be too close;
his body would touch mine.

I imagine my wedding.
I've pictured the man who might take my father's place
and dance with me, a man like the rabbi
who is kind, gentle, and who loves me.

I want to dance,

but he cannot hold me—

not like that.

I wanted to dance

when my friend took me to the Broken Spoke,

the last old-time country dance hall in Austin.

He sat beside me awkwardly

and bounded for the door the moment

I said we could leave. He must have felt

my fear and discomfort.

That was four years ago,

And still, I cannot dance.

I want to dance.

But when I look at my partner,

I see the man I loved most,

the man I trusted

and feel my body

pinned beneath his.

I smell his sweat and his breath,

I see his slightly crooked teeth

and the bit of egg caught from his breakfast.

And I don't want to dance anymore.

No, that's not true.

I want to dance
like Rumi and Hafiz,
radiant and ecstatic
with love for God.

I want to feel the joy
of moving and being close,
at once intimate
and entirely appropriate.

I want to dance
in the light of trust,
freed from sorrow
and my father's shadow.

I want to dance with you, too, Rabbi—
I do want to dance.

Soul Scream

The night before, the pain was so intense
I thought I might have to go to the hospital.
That's what the gynecologist had told me to do.
But what could they do for me?
They'd give me a drug and send me home.
Band-Aid solutions for a complex problem.
The gynecologist says that I should have surgery.
"If we remove the uterus, we remove the source of the pain."
This is linear thinking. I do not believe it will work.

While I speak with the acupuncturist
on the phone, I realize she too doubts
whether a surgery will give me comfort.
I want to say, "My soul is screaming for a child,"
but do not. It will scream whether my organs
are all in place or have been cut away.

Rabbi said earlier that all this will work out.
He is wrong. It will not be o.k.
because it is not all right now.
I cannot have children.
That ability was stolen from me,
taken by someone who should have wanted
only my greatest happiness.

I am at a loss for a solution.

I lie back down, letting the pain escalate.

I hope that my soul, like a toddler having a fit,

will soon tire of this tantrum

and leave my body be.

Rachav

Rachav slowly opened her door
to Pinchas and Calev, teasing them.
She beckoned to them,
drew them unhurriedly inside,
and seduced them.

Burgeoning breast heaving,
she smiled and winked.
How startled they were to enter
her world so easily!

The ecstatic moment reached,
a knock is heard at the door.
Pinchas and Calev hide high above
and listen as the king enters
Rachav's wide, welcoming embrace.
He too knows the pleasures
of her blossoming lips and heated touch.
When he is done, he withdraws,
taking with him cold lies.

Rachav returns her attention to her favored guests,

who remain enraptured in the peak of pleasure.

Caught in the trap of her wiles,

they offer their oaths to God,

unaware that the boundless expression of Ein Sof

is standing as an illusion before them,

a dance of light made to look

like the body of a whore.

Damaged Vessel

When asked why mourners
should lead a congregation in prayer,
Rabbi Solomon Luria said,
"God prefers damaged vessels."

"Ah!" I sighed, sitting back in my chair.
"No wonder God likes me."

But man, man prefers a different
kind of vessel, bowls that are whole
and beautiful, perfect chalices
that shine in the midday sun
and glimmer in moonlight.

HaShem pours His love into me;
it spills out in stories, poetry,
and acts of kindness, the love
I have for both strangers and friends.

Too bad men don't realize
what treasures they might receive
seeping from the fissures
of a damaged vessel.

Nissan 19

I wish so badly
my father
was still here
every time the 19th of Nissan
comes around.

It is his yahrzeit,
yet I don't pray for my father
like most daughters would.

His memory is no blessing.

Instead, I wish he was here
so I could
take him by the shoulders,
shake him,
look him in the eye,
and tell him how much he hurt me.

It isn't fair he got to die
without knowing the way
he gutted my dreams.

Rabbis and Gynecology

I'm sick, really sick again. Well, it's the same thing
that's been going on the last four years.
Only it's getting worse. It was bad enough
that I should have gone to the hospital
this weekend, but who needs a bill like that?

I want to talk with you, my rabbi,
because I don't know the
best course of action to take.
There are no great or easy choices.
However, women's issues are not
your finest subject. You can't
cover up the uneasiness
behind your eyes.

By the way, I think they should teach
a little less Talmud and a little more
gynecology at rabbinical school.
There's always more talk about
too many babies,
not enough babies,
or problems making babies
in the congregation
than anything some crusty old rabbis
wrote in the Talmud.
But I digress....

The pain is so overwhelming,

my best idea is to break into your office

and lie on your couch, crying in a ball,

until you can come in and say

a Mi Sheberach for me.

If only the pain could be prayed away.

Mostly though, it isn't the problem itself

that weighs on me. I'm just tired of being

this ill and in this much pain.

I'm tired of having my life interrupted.

I'm tired of being misunderstood.

And I'm angry,

ANGRY.

Not that I'm sick,

but that this is simply the physical manifestation

of the same emotional and spiritual issues

I've been grappling with all my life.

When does it stop?

O.K. I get it. I lose!

I lose! I lose!

I don't get to have what I want.

I understand.

Now, can you take the pain away, God,

since the lesson is well-learned?

Oh wait. That almost sounds
like a rabbinical problem –
something we can talk about after all.

Lone Traveler

I exit the departure terminal
elated, tired,
looking forward
to my new adventure.

I wish I had a companion
to share my journey,
to lament the ache in our muscles
and laugh at the funny way
the old man two rows back snored.

I look around the lounge at the sea
of waiting faces. I see no one familiar,
no friend or placard with my name
in bold letters on its face.

I walk heavily to the sherut stand
to make my way to Jerusalem,
a single pilgrim on a well-worn road.

The Heart of Loss

You think you're prepared, knowing
the ones closest to you are going to pass,
watching them age, becoming frail,
suffering.
When the pain starts in earnest,
you suffer with them,
pray for them to go, be released swiftly
to the Collector of Souls.

My grandmother, in her final weeks,
sat upright in her hospital bed,
singing an old song from *Show Boat.*

> "I gets weary
>> Sick of tryin'
>> I'm tired of livin'
>> Feared of dyin'
>> But ol' man river
>> He's rollin' along."

A tiny Jewish woman—
a bright soul—
enslaved to a worn out body.

When I saw her, feeble and tired,
I wanted her to move on to the world to come,
to be with my grandfather again.
I prayed God would make her transition peaceful.

But when she went, and I was

truly without her,

I plunged into an unexpected abyss.

She was the last of the elders

      the last one

         cheering for me,

         caring for me.

She waited for me to come home;

she asked about my days.

She whispered courage,

gave me a place to belong.

She knew the answers to my questions.

Now, she didn't need me anymore

and I finally understood

how much I still needed her.

Praying in Jerusalem

Rabbi Nachman says,
"Do not succumb to despair."

It is hard not to.
The woman beside me is weeping,
whispering her deepest longings
into the Kotel's stones.
I don't need an interpreter to know
I want the same thing she does.
Only in my case,
my prayer has already been answered,
"No."

Pressing my forehead to the stone,
my own tears fall.
I've returned to the Kotel by myself,
on this final day in Jerusalem.
When I came here before,
I was too overwhelmed by this place
to pray.

How could I ask God for help
with the weight of five thousand
years of history pressing on my soul?

I Want a God with Arms

In a certain way,
I understand idol worship.
HaShem can be somewhat
dissatisfying in that He can only
be known by faith and has no form.

I want a god with arms
to whom I can pray
to come down from the heavens
to hold me when I cry.

I want a god with legs
who will run from on high
to protect me
when I am in danger.

I want a god with a heart
who will love me
like Krishna did the gopis;
a god who will let me love him
like Rumi and Hafiz.

I want a god with ears, and eyes, and a mouth,
who can hear me and see me,
a god who will not only listen,
but speak back words of encouragement and hope.

I want a god who is here
and now and full, an embodied god
that I know has as much interest in me
as I do in him.

Praying at the Western Wall

The cool stones against
my forehead were a comfort
after the long, hot walk.

Yet when I looked for words,
I had nothing to say
to God.

Now that I cannot have children,
I find no reason to pray.

The Generosity of Women

The Samburu women do not cry
when they are married off
to men they do not love.
They were given an opportunity
to be flirtatious and free with their bodies
as young teens; when it is time to marry,
thoughts turn to economics
instead of matters of the heart.
"We have no expectation of love,"
　they tell me as we sit together under a large tree.
"Our happiness comes from our children."
"And what of women who can have no children?" I ask.
"Those of us who have many give
　the barren women one or two of our own."

Returning to my tent, I lay on my cot,
imagining what it would be like to
live in a land where women are so generous
that they would give up one of their own children
so that their sisters would not
live with the grief of barrenness.

In Kenya, no woman is bereft of child.
Against this measure of generosity,
how can we consider ourselves the advanced nation?

Ignited

I kindle my chanukiyah in the dark,
intensifying the brightness of the light
each of the candles provides,
illuminating a life
lived mostly in shadow.

This year, a few days before Chanukah,
I was given a tremendous gift.
In receiving that gift,
I felt like I finally got the hug
I never got from my parents,
the gentle consolation
I have waited for all my life.
Now, the light within me is ignited,
a fire of love and potential
put before the bellows.

Chanukah is no longer a small light
flickering in the dark,
it is a blaze of God's goodness.

The gift I was given
was hope.

Broken Treasures

I took the broken bits of me
to show to my rabbi,
not entirely sure whether I could
trust him with them or not.

He took them delicately from my hands:
six inches of knotted fishing line,
sea shell fragments, a bit of kelp,
half a button dropped by a seagull.
He silently examined every shard and scrap,
holding them as if they were treasure.

Liking what he saw, he made me an offer.
He would keep my treasure safe for me.
Though others saw junk, he knew the value
of what he held.

I agreed.

He sprinkled the broken bits with special rabbi dust.
(A little got sprinkled on me too.)
I watched him put my treasure in a hand-carved
antique wooden box with a metallic latch.
Then he slipped it in his breast pocket, out of sight.

I sighed with relief.
I didn't have to carry or watch over
the old stuff anymore.
There was room for the new,
and the rabbi dust, a blessing,
empowered me.

Before I departed,
I reached into my right hip pocket.
From it, I pulled an ancient seed.
The seed was dry, dark brown, and somewhat pitted
with age. I held it out gingerly to the rabbi,
cradling it in the palm of my right hand.
This was my most prized possession,
only I did not know how to make it grow.

The rabbi bent over to see what I offered.
He examined it carefully;
even his wandering eye remained focused.

Closing my hand over the object, he stood erect,
taking me by the other hand
to the little garden behind the house.

With a trowel, he dug a small hole
on the right side of the gate.
I dropped the seed inside.
He sprinkled more rabbi dust, said a prayer,
and covered the seed with soil.
I tamped the earth gently.
He drizzled water from the watering can
the rebbetzin kept on the kitchen window sill.

As we left the garden, I grinned broadly.
I knew nothing planted in that garden
would fail to thrive. I felt my seed grow roots
and sprout a stalk, stretching eagerly skyward.

My soul stretched with it,
no longer afraid to say,
"I can hear God."

Sukkot

I had a sukkah built in my back yard
to celebrate the Festival of Booths,
as commanded by God.
When it was done
and the workers who assembled it were gone,
I took a camping chair to sit in it
in the late afternoon of the first day of the holy day.

I sat there for an hour or so,
looking at the grass and the sky.
I heard the sounds of the birds and squirrels,
felt the breeze on my skin
and the warmth of the sun on my face.
For a while, I was entranced
by the shifting light indicating autumn,
my favorite time of year.

I brought with me the sandwich
I made earlier, thick with organic turkey breast,
lettuce, tomato, some red onion, mayonnaise,
and just a touch of whole grain mustard,
between two soft slices of fresh-baked bread.
It was a masterpiece of a sandwich,
a meal I longed to share,
as one does during Sukkot.

But as I had no one to share it with,
I set it to the side in the grass
and let the ants have it
while I cried.

Then I went into the house and called the workers
who had built the sukkah for me.
I asked them to come back and remove it.
There was no one for me to share the holiday with,
to share the celebration of redemption
or with whom to be "a people."

You can't be a nation all alone.

On Being Childless on Yom HaShoah

"Stay Jewish."
  It was the most important advice
  the grandfather had to give.

  A few hours later while the boy ran
  terrified through the trees, the grandfather
  and all the remaining Jews in the town
  were ushered into the synagogue.
  The doors were locked
  and the building set ablaze.
  No one survived.

  The old man spoke of his grandfather,
  his demeanor changing from that of an aged man
  to a ten year old with nothing but love
  and respect for his elders.
  He spoke softly, this man-boy in front of me,
  sharing his grandfather's parting words
  before he was sent running
  through the forest away from their village.
"Stay Jewish."

  The tears in my eyes spilled over
  as he told his story.
  He spoke in the same pronounced
  accent as my grandmother's cousin Ted.

I could not listen to the rest, my heart
breaking at the unrelenting sadness
in the now elderly man's face.

So, I began to think about myself,
the way most people do
when they are no longer listening
to what's going on around them.

I thought back to the previous Friday night.

During the Kabbalat Shabbat service,
the rabbi always asks
the children come forward
to lead most of the service after the
Barchu. He teases them, seeing who can
say the Kaddish Shalem the fastest.
Of course, Rabbi is always the quickest
and most articulate, but every week
it is fun to see the kids try
to outdo the rabbi.

I wanted to be the parent on the sidelines
beaming with pride as my children sang
the V'ahavta in beautiful high-pitched voices
or screeched in frustration as their tongues
tied in knots and the rabbi outdid them again.

That is what I thought about as the
old man told his tale.

We rose to leave; my thoughts remained on
the only mitzvah that really matters:
perpetuating our people.
Yet my womb is cold;
I am and forever will be without child.

What blame will those lost souls heap on me
for failing to avenge their deaths
by creating a Jewish family?

Unanswered Prayers

The women speak about the mikveh
and its meaning to them.
They speak lovingly about how mikveh
improves their relationships
with their partners and children.

Everyone, that is, except me.
I sit beside the rabbi and sip slowly
from my water glass,
doing everything I can not to cry.

As the women talk about how each month's
mikveh is an opportunity to mourn the life
that failed to grow in their bellies,
I stifle sobs.
When one of them reads a prayer that
infertile women sometimes say,
I pinch myself under the table
to keep the tears at bay.

For twenty years, I said all those prayers,
begged God to send me a child.
But none of it was meant to be.
God pushed away my prayers
as one bats off a fly.
Now, it is too late.
Not even a miracle could give me a baby.

And so I sit and pretend

that I chose for things to work out this way

while my sisters delight in a joy

that my heart will never understand.

Rachel Imeinu

She beckons me,
her voice a whisper
on the Jerusalem breeze.
I look up her address.
She's ten kilometers away,
a straight shot down the road
from my hotel.

Anxiety pricks my skin,
my heart flutters.
It is not rejection I fear;
it is her love.

I hesitate.
I wait for the rabbi
to say it's o.k. to go.

I let fear gnaw
at the soft cartilage
in my chest,
yet when I arrive,
breath comes easily to my lungs;
sweet tears fill my eyes.

At Rachel's kever, I feel
her embrace, encouragement
to pour my needs out to God.

She is beside me,
hand on my head, helping me
vomit up what needs
to be issued.
I ask for
what she was given –
A partner who will love me and,
if not children, at least
a healing in my womb
so that I am no longer
in constant pain.

When my prayers are done,
Rachel Imeinu leaves me,
lips on the plastic cover of her kever,
with a sweet and gentle kiss
shared between mothers and their daughters.

Seige in Av

Two days after our enemies
laid siege to Jerusalem,
I went to the Temple steps,
lay in the ruins, and wept.
Desecrated, decimated,
the smell of war still heavy
in the air. What I would give to have
our beautiful Temple returned to us,
so that we could continue
to glorify God!

Now I lay in bed after the siege
to my body. Opened up,
destroyed, my dreams
in ruins. What I would give
to have had one chance, one opportunity
to be part of the line of transmission,
so we could continue as a people
and not be assimilated
into nothingness.

Simchat Torah Super Hero

Yakov danced up to me
carrying a toy Torah.
"Kiss it!" he commanded,
 holding it out to me.
I smiled, dutifully touching my tallit
to his toy, then to my mouth.
Yakov grinned, then danced on.

Adin dressed up in a superhero outfit.
A superhero for Torah.
Dancing, whirling,
spinning like a dervish
as his Abba guided him
among the revelers.

Shmuel wore his first tzitzit.
They were so long they dragged
on the ground behind him
as he walked the circuits
with the dancers.
He waved an Israeli flag,
using the stick as a sword
to impale his brother Yakov
and procure the favored toy Torah,
which he, too, carried proudly
and asked me to kiss.

The children danced and sang with delight.

Young and old together

exalted in gratitude for Torah.

Our gathering was every bit the celebration

Simchat Torah is meant to be.

The Tempest on the Mountain

God sends me to the mountain.
Shofarot sound
and angels call forth creation
in the midst of a tempest.

Standing alone in the storm,
an angel with the face of a hawk
and four sets of wings
approaches,
reaches into my body,
and rips a handful of hissing snakes
from my womb.

Disinterested in my horror,
the angel proclaims
in the language of birds,
the same betrayal
that makes my womb cold
causes the chaos in creation.

Man, unwilling to prepare
the way for his children
steals their futures
as surely as
my own parents took mine.

I have no response
for the angel,
who throws the snakes to the ground
to die on impact.

We reap what we sow.

Still, God loves us.
I see Him, pulling
the forsaken to His breast,
howling with them
in their tears.

My soul knows what to do.
I drop prostrate to the ground
beside the angel,
dead snakes from my
womb all around,
whispering the prayers
of redemption.

The World Aflame

Traditionally celebrated with enormous bonfires
to symbolize the light the great Kabbalist sages
gave us through their teachings,
Lag BaOmer sets the world aflame.

This year, I will do something different.

When darkness falls in its fullest,
when even the moon is covered
by thick folds of evening cloud,
I will light a hundred pounds of fireworks
in the center of my cul de sac.

Hearing the commotion, all the neighbors,
including the children, will come out to watch
light explode and fall from the heavens.

I will dance like a child, giddy with happiness
for Creation. Then as now,
HaShem's light fills the world
and sparks of divine goodness rain down
in a wash of magical starlight.

After Yizkor

Voice breaking, I try to
        sing
the Musaf Chatzi Kaddish,
looking away from the rabbi,
as he catches my gaze
across the congregation.

I cannot stay.
        Quickly, I
remove my tallit and yarmulke, barely
      w h i s p e r i n g
the beginning of the Amidah.

I run as soon as I
get out of the sanctuary,
        heart pounding
as it did all those years ago.

My thoughts are of you,
        Daddy.

Two hundred and seventeen
months ago, you died.
I still will not say
Kaddish for you.

Now, after Yizkor,
the tears that flow
are not for you, but for
my
broken heart

a prayer
a hope

that with Divine grace
the gift of love
might still remain
for me.

Ahuva

My name,
Constance,
was given to me
by a cruel man
to honor
an unbalanced woman
who, in a drunken episode,
burned herself
to death.

Do I want my life
directed by a command
to be faithful
to those whom I
neither respect
nor love?

I listened
to my heart.

Ahuva
came to mind;
the word
a kiss on my forehead.

How would my life change

if those whom I care about most

called me

"Beloved?"

It is an experiment

I've decided to try.

Meeting God at Midnight

Meeting God at Midnight

Running outside, in the warmth
and the dark, thrusting my arms
upward with joy, eyes rolling
in their sockets in ecstasy.
God is everywhere around me!
I smell God in the crescent-bend of the moon,
taste God in the sound of the cicada,
feel God in the scent of early spring roses.

Opaque Essence!
Why do You hide Yourself
in all of these things?
Come forth, allowing us to
embrace!
I cannot be without You....

Tefillin

I am in love with God!
I can hardly speak, my ecstasy is so great.

The rabbi cries out the Barchu.
Bowing low in supplication,
soul singing, I ask God to sit beside me
to join me and whisper secrets to me
as I share my love and gratitude for life
wrapped safely in my tefillin.

Jewish Renewal

Our brothers and sisters

    do not recognize

  us

     as Jews.

How can this be?

Calling us Nazis.
Jeering,
throwing eggs
at the rabbis and children
who have come to pray.

Watching with tear-filled eyes,
I wonder what the sages would say
if they were alive to observe this
    outrage.
I imagine Akiva and Hillel with
tear-stained cheeks and the
Ba'al Shem Tov

    prostrate

between the group at prayer and
the group at war,

trampled

by the police guards
attempting to keep the peace.

Moshe would mount the
barricade, holding up his staff
commanding that we

stop acting fools,

his voice angry with frustration worse
than the incident with the Golden Calf.

I see them there, our greatest
teachers and leaders
who understood both

compassion

for fellow Jews and

love

for HaShem,

calling for reconciliation over
the chaos and
pressing their faces against the
Kotel stones once we have gone,
weeping for a Jewish Renewal.

The prophets are
never silent.

In God's world,

we all pray

for an end to the pain
and hardship we endure
as a natural part of life and
the callousness of our fellows.

We all

may bring
our sacrifices of tears and song
to the Temple's wall,

each hoping

for the same deliverance;

removal of the

unbearable

distance from Him.

Shofar

Tekiah:
a single blast.
Birth; the beginning of the beginning.
A child before the world has
damaged her.
A people before they have become
a nation.

Shevarim:
three broken notes.
Disappointments tearing the soul
even when engaged in tefillah.

Teruah:
nine staccato bursts in quick succession.
Abuse. Neglect. Rape. Racism. Sexism.
Diaspora. Pogrom. Genocide.
Holocaust.
Individual and nation shattered
beyond tzedakah, beyond tikkun.

Tekiah Gedolah:

one, final, long, loud blast.

Sounding until the Ba'al Tekiah has no more breath to give,

the shofar transforms shards

into mosaic and window,

makes whole

what was once broken

past redemption.

Tekiah.

Shevarim.

Teruah.

Tekiah Gedolah.

At Rosh Hashanah,

the Ba'al Tekiah

sounds the whole of teshuvah

with a single song.

There Must Be Prophesy

For the Lord God does nothing unless He has revealed
His secret to His servants, the prophets —
Amos 3:7

It is an abomination,

Amos warned,

to order the prophets silenced.

Warning and guidance

come direct from the divine

mouth to the prophet's ear.

The prophet must speak it;

she is the foghorn

letting us know

we have gone off course.

We stray dangerously without the nevi'im.

We become petty and hard,

concerned with rules instead

of mercy, charity, and compassion.

We become not a people to be

emulated, but one to be despised.

A true prophet

seeks no followers;

takes no profit;

turns the hearts of the people

always toward Torah;

awaits the moshiach,

preparing the world

with good works,

bringing God's light

to the darkest places.

A prophet speaks the harsh

truth, reveals the consequences of our actions,

yet remembers God

is magnanimous and sympathetic.

Where there is repentance,

there is pardon. Always.

Why is there divine pardon?

There is no need for God to punish us.

God offered us a return to the garden

time and time again.

We plowed it under to put up

a Super-Walmart

and a cemetery.

All our prophets can do

is stand in shadow and wail, hoping

they will be allowed to speak

once more.

Shabbat

Voices lifted in song,
setting the Shabbat candles aflame
using only the power of our prayers.

The Ari's Outlook

Enveloped in mist.
Drenched in heavy rain.
The tour guide stands
in the courtyard
talking about the Ari.

I push forward,
nudging my way through
the gate, past the others
until I am at the far side
of the small courtyard
in front of the Ari Ashkenaz shul.

I turn my back to everyone
to look out
into the clouds that cloak
the mountains.
That is where the Ari is.
That is where he found
his inspiration – looking
toward the sea.

I feel them here, the great sages
of Tsfat, standing behind me.
In a dream, the Besht said
they would speak to me
if I asked them to – but I do not ask.

It is enough they are here
and we are together,
straining toward visions
our eyes cannot take in,
waiting for the Shechinah to come.

Kotel

He is an old man,
with a gray beard that reaches
to the middle of his chest.
He hurls insults and sometimes
bottles
at the women,
his gnarled finger pointing
accusation.

He is a young man
in a blue police uniform,
demanding the women
keep their voices
down
because their singing
is an affront to the
men.

He is a child
wearing peyes, tzitzit, and a black felt hat.
He does his best to act like a man,
jeering at women older than his mother,
women
to whom he should show
deference and respect.

She is an old woman.

She slips a tiny piece of paper

between the stones for blessing.

On the paper, she has written

her sister's name: the one

who was little more than a baby

when she died of exposure

in her mother's arms,

worth not even a bullet.

She is a student from America

with thick red hair and bright blue eyes.

She arrived in Jerusalem to pray

but her heart is torn.

Unable to pray with tefillin, tallit and a Torah

as she does at home, she stands

at the rear of the plaza

and weeps.

She is an activist.
She holds tight to her Torah
while men curse her and
police try to
rip
the scroll from her grasp.
Will she spend three years in prison
for the crime of wanting
to talk to God?

Rabbi Rabinowitz,
answer me this question:
do the ultra-Orthodox really believe
my prayers are less pleasing to God
because I am a woman?

Swept Away

While the women pray,
two men pull scraps
of prayer from cracks
in the old stone wall,
throwing them to the floor,
sweeping them away.

So many prayers.
Hundreds of hopes.
Thousands of dreams.
Only trash now.

The women pray on,
unmoved.

Yom Kippur

The gates flung open wide,
My body sat and stood as
commanded in the synagogue,
while my spirit lay prostrate before God.

Walking into the synagogue
the previous evening for Kol Nidre,
my heart's prayer was for death,
for the courage to end a life
filled with beauty and incredible pain.

I offered my self-pity as a sacrifice
before the gates,
before God.
I lay there with my brokenness.
I prayed.
I wept.
I waited.

Face down in the dust, I listened,
my white tallit wrapped around me,
less a shroud than a comfort,
a blanket for my soul.

I heard the martyrs' footsteps.
The rabbi told their stories as they ran by,

racing through the gates I feared to breach.

Rabbi Akiva stopped and knelt beside me.

Before walking through

he whispered in my ear, "Enter."

The shofar sounded the closing of the gates.

I had two choices:

remain on the ground,

outside and away from God

or stand and run through.

I hesitated.

As the gates slowly closed,

I felt a sense of panic;

I did not want to be left behind,

left without God.

I heard the rabbi say,

"The lamp of God is the spirit of a man."

My own being's light surged,

longing to be with its Source.

Jumping from my prostration, I raced forward

and slipped in an instant before

the gates slammed shut.

I turned to look back.

My self-pity lay abandoned
on the other side.

I looked at it there,
a small cardboard box
wrapped in greasy, crinkled
brown paper.
Like a suitcase forgotten on a dock,
bereft after its ship has left port.

I heard the whisper, "Choose life."
My heart's flame kindled again,
the light that flickers
when it wants to go home.

A Kiss at the Gate

At the end of the Ne'ilah service
when the gates of heaven are closing
and the Sefer Chayim is sealed for another year,
the rabbi asks anyone who wants to,
to join him on the amud.

But to his eldest son, he says, "You—
I want you up here with me."
The sixteen year old complies
while the congregants laugh and smile.

Together, the two men walk to the center
of the stage where the parochet is still open.
Gently, the elder man kisses the younger on the side of the face
and hugs him around the shoulders. He looks with absolute love
upon his son. The son accepts his father's affection.

They stand in the sight of God, praying
shoulder to shoulder.

Mercy Gate

Standing outside the Golden Gate
in Jerusalem's old city,
I bow my head to weep.

If the stones here could talk,
they would speak of the unending
sadness of the Jewish people,
their enduring hope
for a time of security and redemption,
of a peace
only the moshiach can bring.

Beside me, unseen, the Shechinah
stands, also weeping.
She cries for my inability to feel
HaShem's mercy, which is given
freely along with His justice.

Creation

In the darkness
where God is everything and nothing,
where there was no division
between what was, is and will be,
in the space
before time yet
enveloped by time,
where God is
whole and absolute,
present and complete,
but entirely unknowable,
I stood
waiting for creation;
praying God would choose
to know God's-self and
in the process be known
by an ant like me.

Watching and waiting,
my prayer was answered.
Light cascaded, sparks
erupted from the center
of nothing-ness as God contracted,
imploding, expelling, radiating
goodness and possibility
from absolute unity to the division
that is the universe.

Behind this light streaked the angels,
shofarot blaring,
singing Creation
into being, a chorus
of words so beautiful,
I could not help but cry.

Then, magnificently, from the
navel of the void
came the Merkabah
streaming behind it the greatest
of God's gifts, Shefa and Neshamah –
a literal river of abundance and life
emanating in all directions.

Tree of Life

Rooted in sky,
drinking from the waters
beyond the rakiyah,
branches outstretched
toward Earth,
Eitz Chayim
drips shefa in
succulent, sugared orbs.
Fruit dangling just out of reach,
I stand on my toes,
levitating upon the teachings,
the sages,
Torah;
my heart blossoms,
opening to the sunshine
of HaShem's abiding love, the shade
of His unending mercy.

Date Palm

Milk and honey.

Dates.

Bees.

Sun.

Rain.

Israel.

Each one God's gift.

In the Torah,

Israel is referred to

as the land of

milk and honey.

In our history,

honey comes not from bees,

but from dates.

How do I know?

I look into the

date farmer's eyes

when he talks

about his trees.

Egalitarian Prayers

Having come from the
women's side of the Kotel
where singing is prohibited,
my heart leapt.

They were everything I
don't care for at home,
a bunch of kibbutzniks,
weathered by the sun,
sitting in a circle
singing in a summer camp style.

The charedim watched them,
men and women singing together,
letting them be.

Had I known the words,
I'd have joined their singing,
but it was enough for
my heart to feel
the kavanah behind the song.

I Write in English

The old professor pulled me aside,
engaging me in conversation about Israel.
Without him and his wife and Ben Gurion and all
the others whose photos are displayed in his home,
there might be no Jewish state at all.
But he is elderly now and has lost touch
with the realities of our daily lives.

"You write in English!" he exclaimed,
turning his eyes to the ground.
He spat, heavily and noisily,
giving me an old Yiddish curse for good measure.
"How can you be a Jew and write in English?"

"I don't know. How can I be a Jew and
write in Aramaic or Greek or Ladino?
How can I be a Jew and write in Jewish-Arabic
which in various forms has been spoken for more
than a thousand years from Egypt to Iraq to Morocco?
How can I write in German or Russian or Yiddish,
the languages my family may have used for their
final prayers before being turned to dust in the ovens?"
Out of deference to the professor's contribution
to our world, I keep these words to myself.

But despite my birth in North America

and my disinterest in making aliyah,

make no mistake, Professor – I am a Jew.

I am an American woman who wears tefillin

and studies with a *Conservative* rabbi –

yes, a real rabbi even if you do not consider him such.

I spend my Shabbats in shul

and many of my evenings in minyan.

I carry the Torah, parading it through

the congregation for all to see,

and have been given the honor of Hagba'ah,

something few women are able to do.

When I lift the scroll high for all to see,

I feel lifted on top of the world. I

P – R – O – U – D – L – Y

wear a Magen David as big as a silver dollar,

knowing such a display could get me killed.

And yes, though I've never set foot on Eretz Yisrael,

I am a Jew.

I write in English

because more than half the Jews in the world

do not read Hebrew.

I write in English
because those who seek to oppress us
read English.

I write in English
because I will not be controlled or marginalized
by an orthodoxy that seeks to dominate women.

I write in English
because I want the Jews who assimilate to know
you don't have to be a Yeshivite to be a Jew.

I write in English
because I seek a direct line to God,
to write as it is HaShem directs
…and though it may disappoint you,
when HaShem suggests words to put down on the page,
those words come not in Hebrew,
but in English.

Curse me all you want, Professor,
but I am American Jewry
and I will always
write in English.

Tikvah

Last night, in an unrelated context,
the rabbi mentioned the word, *tikvah*.
Immediately, I thought of Hatikvah,
the beautiful anthem of Eretz Yisrael.

A homeland.
Israel.
What was it like
in a world with no Jewish home?

Admittedly, I am a fatted calf,
enjoying the relative safety of the
"land of the free and the home of the brave."
Yet there is no denying our history:
Spanish Jews lazed happily
in the heat of the Spanish sun
for the centuries before the Inquisition;
Babylonian Jews basked
in great liberty and learning.

Is there any country
where the proverbial trains
won't come for us,
that we won't have to flee,
barefoot and penniless?

Today, there is tikvah, hope.

My brethren guard the borders there,

stand ready to open her doors.

A Flower in Jerusalem

A flower holds tight
to the city wall.
A delicate thing,
five small white petals
on a thin stalk,
gripping stone,
intent on survival.

There it was
on my morning walk
through the Old City.
In the early evening,
I came back to it, engrossed,
needing to know
whether it had survived
the afternoon's rainstorm.

The flower was there, still
wet and beaten, full
of life purpose.

Smiling, I stopped in a shop
for an American-style coffee,
weak and insipid by Middle Eastern standards,
but a comforting taste of home.
When I had had my fill,
I walked to my hotel,
past the wall where my
flower had been.

It was gone, picked
silently by the Shechinah,
too alluring to be left alone.

Tisha B'Av

Peering through the woven
metal mechitza at the Kotel,
I strain to see whether or not
my friend
is on the other side.

Seeing only glimpses of men,
I wonder…is that his
>
> beard
>
> neck
>
> profile?

They all have on white shirts
black pants, as he would.

Did he wear his hat?

Can I hear his voice?

Then yes.
Perhaps.
I think it could be.

But in a moment,
the man is gone
and I remain alone
with my prayers
in the women's section

where we are not
allowed to sing.

In the Brilliance of the Light

In the brilliance of the light
emanating from Source,
I fall to my knees, trembling.
There is no smell, taste, or sound,
only light,
holding all potential.

It is in this form, this space,
God decided what would be.
Angels will be born in this light.
God's essence will come forth
to share the words
He will have me speak,
words I must express
or let die in the silence.

In that moment of nothing
and everything, in the presence
of the Divine Essence,
in the waiting for the manifestation
of all, my thoughts turn to you.
My spirit calls out your name if
only so I will not be alone
to bear witness
to this incredible knowing of God.

A Wink of the Moon

Standing in the middle
of the street on a mid-summer
night, I looked up at the sky.
Thinking of you. So far away.
Were you gazing toward the heavens,
taking in the same stars?

While I stood there,
I was reminded by the
stars' twinkling light
that in life and death
we are all made of stardust,
particles HaShem sent
flying through the universe
at the time of Creation,
imbuing the living with the spark
of life and the dead with gifts
we cannot comprehend.
When we recognize we are
nothing less than a divine gift,
the sadness of loss can be
transformed into compassion
and prayers for those
who cannot yet see.

Wanting you to know that wishes
for blessings and healing
were traveling to you on the light
from those distant stars, I waved
my fingers at the moon,
making it wink.
Hoping you would see this
unnatural phenomenon and
understand my astronomical message.

My Cat Ziva

Ziva has one
strange quirk.

When I speak in English,
she is indifferent.
When I speak in Spanish,
she lolls on the bed, sleepily.
When I speak in Yiddish,
she perks up an ear,
but soon looks away.
Hebrew, though—Hebrew
is more interesting to her
than kitty treats.

Upon hearing Hebrew,
Ziva runs around the room
in delight and throws herself
on the ground in ecstasy.

When I read or sing aloud in Hebrew
she runs over to me
to put her head in my mouth
as if to see where the sound
is coming from.

When I lay my tefillin
and don my tallit, she dances
around me, like Miriam
(only without the timbrels).

Maybe she is Elijah.
It would not be unlike him
to sneak around
in a magnificent disguise, but...

if Elijah is stuck
in the body of a little cat,
we must have quite
a wait for the coming
of the moshiach.

I Talk With God

I talk with God
and God talks back.
There, I said it out loud.
It happens in prayer;
enraptured, I fall
trembling to the floor
freeing my spirit to soar
into the heavens.

I meet God in a garden,
where the lip of the
forest rests against a meadow.
We talk like friends.
We talk like lovers.
We talk like children.

Unless we don't talk
and just sit together,
enjoying one another's
company in silence.

I See an Old Woman

I see an old woman at the table next to mine.
She sits in a wheelchair, white head
not quite comfortably high enough over the table;
she eats quietly. Her family chatters around her.

I catch her eye and smile.
She embodies everything I miss
about my grandmother.

We had good times together.
We treated ourselves to lunches at the Polo Lounge
where we watched celebrities and kvetched
about the overpriced fare, listened
to the news and discussed politics, always siding
with those who advocate social justice. We read
the *Number One Ladies Detective Agency* series together—
she savored each word on the page,
I listened to the stories as I ran errands—
then shared our thoughts over dinner.

I see an old woman at the table next to mine.
She smiles back, and tears come to my eyes.
I hope my grandmother can see me
through this woman's eyes, feel my love
for her as she enjoys her place
in the Olam Ha-Ba.

A Rabbi Is Only A Man

The rabbi sat front and center
at the burial of his father.
To his left sat his aunt, his father's sister,
to his right, the youngest of his sons.

I watched him in his grief,
providing comfort and love
to his family. A private man,
he did not break down,
but despite his restraint
his sadness could not be contained.
It radiated from his eyes and skin
with the force of a heat shimmer
in the desert. When he spoke,
the rabbi sometimes joked
and sometimes shared a bit of the sadness
spilling through the rent in his shirt.

Seeing him as a mourner
and a man among men,
my heart broke. I wished
I had more to offer
than my own weak comfort,
donuts and warm smiles. I wished
the rabbi could somehow be granted
immunity from life's sorrows.

Girl Scout Cookies

Today, we met at the synagogue
to discuss a service project
that would bring clean water
to a village in Africa.

Like any good Jew,
I brought a box of cookies
to the meeting.
Girl Scout cookies.
The kind you can't get your hands on
for at least another month.
I mean, how can one talk about
drought and hunger in Africa
without a little snack?

No one touched them.
As the meeting progressed,
I thought to myself,
"What is wrong with these people?
Since when don't Jews eat Thin Mints?
I could sell them for gold."

Still perplexed when the meeting adjourned,
I left the cookies unopened
on the conference room table.

"Today was a fast day,"

a friend said to me ten hours later.

I thought I might die.

Could I be a bigger schlemiel?

And yet, no one had pointed out my mistake.

Through my embarrassment, I had to smile.

Kindness had prevailed

in my community's silence.

Himmelfahrtstrasse

In the hard packed earth
of the death camp Sobibor,
a Jewish archaeologist is finding
the exact paving materials used
for the Nazi's "Road To Heaven,"
Himmelfahrtstrasse.

Mixed with the dirt
are metal Magen Davids,
keys, watches,
the tiny identification tag
of a six year old girl...
babies' unheard giggles,
the sighs of the old;
the terror of parents
who could not protect;
young women's aspirations
to have children of their own...

the ash and dreams
of a quarter million souls.

Prayers without Tefillin

God knocks politely
on the inside of my skull
at the place where my tefillin rests
above and between my eyes.

Hearing His whisper, His lover's call,
I laugh.
God has a terrible sense of timing.

I am on an airplane
bound for Tel Aviv,
surrounded by men who would riot
if they saw me remove from their pouch
the small black boxes
I prize so greatly,
now hidden inside my bag.

I smile.
God will have to wait
for tomorrow, for Haifa, in
my hotel room where we can
be alone.
Until then, all the knocking
is just giving me a headache,
a call to prayer
I cannot answer.

Meeting Ezekiel

Ezekiel is a bit like the
caterpillar in *Alice in Wonderland*.
A young man with a joyful countenance,
wise and strange,
he sat smoking a hookah
when I finally found him in a dream.

He greeted me like family,
whispered an incantation
into me so that I could understand
his speech and the visions
he would share. Patting the ground
beside him, he beckoned me to sit
and ask my questions.

"When will Israel once more
hear HaShem speak?"
I asked. The prophet
blew smoke rings from either
side of his mouth.
I wanted to know if,
as at Sinai, all Israel would again
hear God's voice.

"Ah," Ezekiel said,

smiling at the question.

He threw his hands

into the air, creating

a whirlwind before us.

In it were all manner

of people and things:

idols,

lovers,

fires,

war planes,

newborn babies,

laughing children,

corpses.

I looked at Ezekiel,

uncomprehending.

He smiled,

waved the cyclone away,

and laughed heartily

at his private joke

before he took up his hookah

and disappeared.

In the Light of the Chanukah Candles

On this, the sixth night of Chanukah,
the rabbi reminded the community
that the lighting of our chanukiyot
is a public act, a testament
to our reliance upon
and dedication to HaShem.

To kindle the candles
is also to bring our best,
often hidden selves into the light,
to take that which we conceal
and show it proudly
for all the world to see.

Jewish identity is not
only about defiance
in the face of those
who would slaughter us.
Being a Jew is about loving God
in ways small and great
and not being ashamed
to rely on HaShem.

There is only one God,

the God of Abraham,
the singular God with many names,
who has inscribed those names upon our hearts
and wishes for us to share its meaning
in the light of the Chanukah candles.

Angels

I am the only one who can see them,
two angels in the tree outside
the room where we study.
They are drawn by the sounds
of Hebrew and ancient Aramaic.

As the rabbi haphazardly tosses out words,
the angels draw their swords, mouths open
slightly, ready to move against us.
I keep my eyes trained outside
while I listen to the rabbi.

I go to the class to protect it.
With force of will, I place a barrier
around us. Heat pours from
my body as I work to keep us safe.
The angels react to this, leaping
from branch to branch
in the enormous old tree
where they stand guard.

Their eyes are black,
their wings folded.
They do not love or hate, only act.
HaShem gave the edict long ago that
man is to travel to the higher places
only when called.

I know Rabbi is not
really teaching Kabbalah,
merely topics related to it,
only asking the brain to consider
HaShem in different ways.

Eventually, the rabbi turns his attention to
other matters, stops using the words
that pull the angels from the heavens.

I lean back in my chair,
exhausted. It is dark now,
and we are safely able to go home.

God Whispers Thunder

Substance against the dark.
God is my constant companion,
the gentle glow that gives shadow.

My soul reaches
through the darkness
to catch the word
God whispers
softly
just beyond my grasp.

I draw nearer, lips apart,
quivering, waiting
for a phrase like honey.
God's sweet speech compels me.

I listen more intently,
I give myself over entirely
to God's invitation.

I will have no other.
The whisper turns
into the roar of a breaking storm,
a victorious howl, embracing me
in thunder.

A Joyful Yom Kippur

The rabbi announced at Rosh Hashanah
that we were going to have
a joyful Yom Kippur.
I didn't respond,
but thought to myself
the guy has lost his mind.
Yom Kippur
is a day of tears,
a day to be sorry
for all we've done wrong.

During the seemingly endless
recitations of the Vidui
and of course in Yizkor,
there was time for tears,
to feel the gravity of not only
personal sin
but humanity's too.
There were moments I wobbled
from the weight of our evil.

But during the last confession of faith,
before the final recitation of the Vidui,
the rabbi led us in raucous celebration.
We sang and banged our machzorim
and the backs of our pews,
stomping our feet in jubilation.

As the gates closed,
I understood the rabbi's exultation.
I knew in all my being
our sins had been forgiven.

When Yom HaShoah Ends

"What do we do tomorrow?"
   the rabbi asked as we came
   together for Yom HaShoah.
   We were a smaller gathering
   than in years past. Online newspapers
   questioned commemorating the Shoah
   outside Yom Kippur's Yizkor,
   or perhaps Tisha B'Av,
   now that the survivors are passing away.

"What do we do tomorrow?"
   I listened to stories of
   Muslims who saved Jews in
   Morocco and Tunisia,
   stories that have significance
   in a time when most stories
   of Jews and Muslims together
   teem with dissension, mistrust, and hatred.

"What do we do tomorrow?"
   First, we have to ask ourselves,
   "What didn't we do yesterday?"

I thought of my grandmother's Bavarian cousin
who was visiting the U.S. when WWII began.
He never saw his family again.
I recalled his tears and inability to speak
about those who died.

I thought of my bubbie and her
sadness over her lost family.
My uncle and mother ached to tell her
they'd found and met a single cousin
who'd escaped to Israel,
but Bubbie was already gone.

I thought of Europe's rising tide of anti-Semitism,
of Holocaust deniers and neo-Nazis right here in Texas,
the swarms of police that protect us
when we gather at the shul.

I thought of my Rwandan friend,
a Hutu whose Tutsi husband perished;
with all his family
in the genocide.
She was left to raise
their two small children.

"What do we do tomorrow?"
  We stand up together and
  loudly say "Never Again"
  as a call for all people.

We demand action from leaders
who would watch others perish because
"It doesn't affect my constituents."

We open our doors at every opportunity
to the "Other"— and shout at their pursuers
that we will not allow their hatred
to enter our homes.

We hide those who must be hidden.
We bribe those who must be bribed.
We quiet and comfort those who need more
than our good wishes and prayers.

We must all do this,
even at the cost of our own lives.

Tomorrow, we end this –
and when it is done for everyone,
we can stop commemorating
Yom Ha Shoah.

Glossary

Abba: Hebrew for "father."

Ahuva: given name meaning "beloved."

Aliyah: Hebrew for "to ascend," in this context, to move to Israel.

Amidah: Hebrew for "standing," the core prayer of the Jewish service.

Amud: lectern from which the cantor leads prayers.

Ari: Hebrew for "lion," the Ari refers to Isaac Luria (1534-1572), an important rabbi from the mystical tradition in Tsfat. He's considered the father of contemporary Kabbalah.

Ari Ashkenaz Shul: synagogue in Tsfat, Israel where the Ari prayed. The congregation was well known for welcoming Shabbat in a field (now a courtyard) outside the synagogue.

Av: a month in the Jewish calendar. Av is the Hebrew root of "father."

Ba'al Shem Tov: Hebrew for "Master of the Good Name," the Ba'al Shem Tov was the name used for Rabbi Yisroel ben Eliezer (1698-1760), a Jewish mystical rabbi. Also called the Besht.

Ba'al Tekiah: a person who blows the shofar.

Barchu: part of the Jewish prayer service, considered by some to be a call to prayer.

Ben Gurion: (1886-1973) a prominent founder and Prime Minister of the state of Israel.

Besht: the "nickname" given to the Ba'al Shem Tov using the first letters of Ba'al Shem Tov.

Bible: the Hebrew Bible, consisting of three parts, Torah (teachings), Nevi'im (prophets) and Ketuvim (writings). The Hebrew Bible is also known by the acronym Tanakh.

Bimah: elevated platform on which the Torah is read.

Bubbie: Yiddish word for "grandmother."

Chanukah: Jewish holy day that begins near the end of the month of Kislev and is celebrated for eight nights. Chanukah is Hebrew for "dedication," reminding us of the rededication of the holy Temple in Jerusalem after the Jewish victory over the Greeks in 165 BCE.

Chanukiyah/Chanukiyot: a nine-branched candelabra lit ceremonially during the holy days of Chanukah.

Charedim: term that refers to ultra-orthodox Jews.

Chatzi Kaddish: Kaddish, Aramaic for "holy," a transitional prayer that characterizes God's holiness. Chatzi, meaning "half," refers to the shortest version.

Ein Sof: a reference in the Lurianic Kabbalah to the infinite God in God's most transcendent and indescribable state.

Eitz Chayim: Hebrew for "Tree of Life," also refers to a Torah scroll.

Elijah: a prophet and miracle worker during the 9th century BCE.

Eretz Yisrael: Hebrew for the "Land of Israel."

Golden Gate: oldest of the gates in Jerusalem's Old City walls. The Shechinah was thought to appear through this gate, and will again when the moshiach comes.

Hafiz: Sufi mystical poet.

Hagba'ah: lifting the Torah scroll at the end of the Torah service.

HaShem: Hebrew for "The Name," it is a deferential term for "God."

Hatikvah: Hebrew for "the hope," it is the Israeli national anthem. The lyrics were adapted from a poem by Naphtali Herz Imber.

Hillel: (110 BCE-10 CE) a famous Jewish sage and leader; associated with the redacted Oral Law, the Talmud (Mishnah and Gemara).

Hookah: water pipe.

Imeinu: Hebrew for "our mother," an honorific term for Jewish matriarchs.

Kabbalah: Hebrew for "receiving," Kabbalah is a Jewish mystical tradition that seeks to understand how the universe and life work. Kabbalah is an esoteric system of interpreting Jewish scripture.

Kabbalat Shabbat: Hebrew for "welcoming/receiving the Sabbath." This is a prayer service that joyfully welcomes the Sabbath, chanted or sung before the more solemn Ma'ariv service.

Kabbalist Sage: ancient expert in Kabbalah known as m'kubal (receiver).

Kaddish Shalem: Kaddish, Aramaic for "holy," and Shalem, meaning "whole or complete," is a transitional prayer that characterizes God's holiness. This prayer is often said after the Amidah.

Kavanah: Hebrew for "direction of the heart" or intentionality.

Kever: grave or tomb.

Kibbutzniks: people who live in a collective community (kibbutz) in Israel.

Kol Nidre: prayer recited in the synagogue at the beginning of the Yom Kippur evening service. The prayer's purpose is to release individuals from their unmet vows.

Kotel: known as the Wailing or Western Wall, it was once a rampart of the Temple in Jerusalem.

Krishna: a Hindu god.

Kvetch: Yiddish for to "complain" or "whine."

Ladino: Judeo-Spanish language.

Lag BaOmer: a festive holy day falling between Passover and Shavuot, the period during which the days are counted (the counting of the Omer). The 33rd day of the Omer. An "omer" is an ancient measure of grain.

Machzor(im): the prayer books used during the High Holy Days.

Magen David: Shield of David, in the form of a six pointed star representing Judaism and the Jewish People.

Maimonides: Moses ben Maimon (1139-1204 CE), the greatest Jewish philosopher and rabbinic scholar of the medieval period; author of the *Mishneh Torah,* among other texts.

Mechitza: partition or separation used in traditional synagogues and other religious sites to keep men and women from being distracted by or mingling with each other.

Mercy Gate: see Golden Gate.

Merkabah: the chariot that Ezekiel saw in his visions. Also refers to a school of Jewish mysticism.

Mi Sheberach: a prayer generally said for the healing of the ill.

Mikveh: ritual bath.

Minyan: gathering of 10 Jews (traditionally, only males) that enables the recitation of certain prayers in traditional services.

Mitzvah: commandment, a mandated behavior.

Moshe: Moses.

Moshiach: Hebrew for "the anointed one," the messiah, who has not yet come.

Ne'ilah: the final service during Yom Kippur.

Neshamah: Hebrew for "spirit" or "breath."

Nevi'im: prophets.

Nissan: month of the Hebrew calendar, usually around April on the Gregorian calendar.

Olam Ha-Ba: refers to "the world to come."

Old City: the walled city in the center of modern Jerusalem.

Parochet: curtain or screen that covers the (Torah) ark.

Peyes: uncut portions of hair by/before the ears worn by some groups of ultra-orthodox men.

Rabbi: teacher; modern leader of a synagogue.

Rabbi Akiva: Akiva ben Yosef (40-137 CE), one of the most heroic Jewish scholars and martyrs.

Rabbi Nachman: (1772-1810 CE) founder of the Breslov Chasidic movement.

Rabbi Rabinowitz: (1970- present) rabbi who oversees the Kotel activities in Jerusalem.

Rabbi Solomon Luria: (1510-1573 CE) one of the greatest decisors of Ashkenazic Jewish law.

Rakiyah: the veil or barrier between the waters in the heavens and the earth below.

Rebbetzin: a rabbi's wife.

Rosh Hashanah: Jewish New Year; the beginning of the High Holy Days.

Rumi: Persian mystical poet.

Samburu: Nilotic people of north-central Kenya, related to the Maasai.

Schlemiel: Yiddish word for a bungler whose awkwardness can cause damage.

Sefer Chayim: Hebrew for "Book of Life," referring allegorically to the "book" inscription that, during the High Holy Days, seals the fate of each person for the coming year.

Shabbat: Sabbath, the Jewish day of rest.

Shechinah: feminine aspect of God; connotes the dwelling of the Divine Presence with the Jewish People generally and within the Jerusalem Temple specifically.

Shefa: abundance.

Shema: Hebrew for "Listen!" The three-part Jewish declaration of faith, reward and prohibition.

Sherut: shared-ride taxi in Israel.

Shevarim: staccato note blown on the shofar.

Shoah: Holocaust.

Shofar(ot): musical instrument made of a horn, used for communal religious purposes.

Shul: Yiddish for "school." Today it refers to a synagogue.

Simchat Torah: holy day celebrating yearly completion of the Torah reading.

Sinai: the mountain on which the Ten Commandments were given to Moshe; also the place where the Israelites truly become a people.

Sukkah: humble, temporary outdoor dwelling, used during the festival Sukkot, to commemorate the Israelites' time wandering in the desert.

Sukkot: the Festival of Booths, a festival commemorating the forty-year period of wandering in the desert; also a harvest festival.

Synagogue: Jewish place of worship.

Tallit: ritual prayer shawl with fringes (tzitzit).

Talmud: the central text of rabbinic Judaism, it is a compilation of "Oral Torah," also known as the Mishnah and Gemara; the text contains legal process, law (halacha) and stories (aggada).

Tefillah: Hebrew for "prayer," often specifically refers to the Amidah.

Tefillin: known as phylacteries, small boxes into which sacred texts have been inserted. Tefillin are worn on the head and arm during certain prayer services, particularly in the morning, except on Shabbat and holy days.

Tekiah: singular note blown on the shofar.

Tekiah Gedolah: a maximally-extended note blasted on the shofar.

Temple: the central Jewish holy site in Jerusalem, destroyed at the beginning of the Common Era.

Teruah: type of two-note arrangement blown on the shofar.

Teshuvah: Hebrew for "return," generally used to describe repentance.

Tikkun: Hebrew for "repair," the process of fixing or transforming.

Tikvah: Hebrew word for "hope."

Tisha B'Av: the 9th day of the month of Av, an annual fast day commemorating the destruction of the first and second Temples, in addition to other catastrophes.

Torah: Hebrew for "teach," the Torah comprises the Five Books of Moses and contains the 613 commandments (mitzvot).

Tsfat: a town in northern Israel where many important Jewish teachers and mystics once lived. Also spelled Safed.

Tzedakah: Hebrew for "righteousness," this term refers to charitable giving. However a "tzadik" is not only charitable, but a righteous and learned person.

Tzitzit: in today's parlance, ritual fringes worn on four-cornered garments traditionally worn by men. Tzitzit are also found on tallitot, worn during prayer services.

V'ahavta: Hebrew for "and you shall love," the word beginning the first paragraph of the Shema.

Vidui: the confession of transgressions said many times throughout Yom Kippur services.

Yahrzeit: Yiddish for "a year's time," refers to the anniversary of the death of a loved one/family member for which the "Mourner's Kaddish" is traditionally recited, and a candle is lit on behalf of the departed.

Yarmulke: also known as "kippah," a head covering worn by Jewish men.

Yeshivite: a person who studies at a yeshiva, a Jewish institution focused on intensive study of rabbinic texts.

Yiddish: the historic, German-related language of Ashkenazi Jews.

Yizkor: Hebrew for "remembrance," this is the memorial service recited at particular times during the year.

Yom HaShoah: Holocaust Remembrance Day.

Yom Kippur: The Day of Atonement, the holiest day of the Jewish year and the last of the High Holy Days.

Ziva: a female given name meaning "splendor."

Biography

Ahuva Batya [Constance] Scharff, PhD, is the Senior
Addiction Research Fellow and Director of Addiction
Research at Cliffside Malibu Treatment Center and coauthor
of the bestselling book, *Ending Addiction for Good*. She is
also an international speaker on the topic of substance abuse,
a volunteer with Jewish Family Services of Austin, and an
afternoon minyan leader at her synagogue, Congregation
Agudas Achim in Austin, Texas.